Stephanie Luna grew up in Hutchinson, Kansas. Cooking is not her forte, but when she makes a mean batch of tortillas, siblings say they taste just like their late mother's which is an honor. She currently lives in Wichita, Kansas, with her husband, Mike, and their brat cat, Julia. Stephanie's compassion for people and love for encouraging students are the reasons why she was an educator for a community college in Kansas and an online university for several years. Direct and indirect experiences in this collection of poems are sure to inspire the reader to pick up her book.

For my parents, Luis and Ruth Luna, who rest quite comfortably in the Heavens above. My husband, Mike, siblings and other relatives who have all encouraged me to keep pushing myself to succeed. My nieces and nephews, because I want them to realize they can meet and exceed the goals they set out to achieve. My great friends, colleagues and customers who offer me a different outlook on life every day.

Stephanie Luna-Allala

Situetry: Living in Pandemica

Austin Macauley Publishers™
London • Cambridge • New York • Sharjah

Ordering Information
Quantity sales: Special discounts are available on quantity purchases by corporations, associations, and others. For details, contact the publisher at the address below.

Publisher's Cataloging-in-Publication data
Luna-Allala, Stephanie
Situetry: Living in Pandemica

ISBN 9781638293620 (Paperback)
ISBN 9781638293637 (e-Pub e-book)

Library of Congress Control Number: 2022919719

www.austinmacauley.com/us

First Published 2022
Austin Macauley Publishers LLC
40 Wall Street,33rd Floor, Suite 3302
New York, NY 10005
USA

mail-usa@austinmacauley.com
+1 (646) 5125767

My husband, Mike, who had to endure listening to all my dreams, goals, and accomplishments. Mom and Dad who both rest quite comfortably in His Paradise. My siblings, nieces, nephews, other relatives, friends, co-workers, and all who have influenced me.

Table of Contents

Enemy Revelation

Forced into adulthood
Earlier than many knew
High school seniors
Felt less than leaders
The world's been turned
Upside down, look around
Schools and businesses closed
New life is opposed
Introvert life became the norm
Still people are bored
Constant handwashing
And staying six-feet apart
Only goes so far
This revelation is a genesis
One we would rather exodus
To the young, old, and compromised
Trust we will once again rise

A new year brought us a new sense – whether it was someone's two cents, sense of fear, sense of compassion, or sense of division, we all gained a new mode of living that helps guide us into a world of turmoil. We continue to live a new style, yet one that is far from a new world order, so never fear change. Things just seem different because we all experienced comfort interpreted in our own ways until one day it seemed like an anvil came swooshing in the air and right against our heads.

C'mon, is it really that bad to wash hands more than usual? Is it really that bad to wear masks or other styles of mouth coverings to stabilize germs? More importantly, is it that bad to request of friends, family, acquaintances, and strangers to do for you if you are doing for them? We must remember that with new change comes a new resourcefulness in how we care for ourselves and how we conduct our daily living practices.

Ask yourself how your norm compares
to the New Norm.

This is a good principle to follow

In a World Lacking Quality Leadership

You may find a few things need
changing but not impossible to do.

Friends and Foes

This you should know
Persistent coughing
Morning, noon, and night
I wouldn't wish this on you
Non-stop headaches and fevers
Congestion and low oxygen levels
Loss of taste and smell
I wouldn't wish this on you
Being hospitalized
Spikes the odds
Of being socially limited
As loved ones cannot visit
I wouldn't wish this on you
Home recuperating with oxygen
Why me? Crying in silence
Bumping into things
From loss of balance
More fevers, nosebleeds,
Pink eye and other ails
Physical therapy makes me fragile
Still can't entirely taste or smell
I moved forward

Humble my experience was
As many others passed on
What is for sure
This is a journey I hope many
Can avoid or destroy

A Story of 'Rona 9Tene

Times were unprecedented
And demented
Layoffs and furloughs triggered
Jobless claims by the millions
That is one hell of a sum
Along with a stimulus of trillions
To keep Americans goin'
No hand sanitizers, wipes, TP
This was an age of famines
No one could ever imagine
Staying home, sheltering in place
Both were one and the same
Missing family and friends
So much we reminisced
As we socially distanced
For the sake of flattening the curve
Which sure got on people's nerves
Those lucky to be more social
Were the Employees Essential
'Rona, you were a colossal novel
That we remain learning from such a debacle
Honoring those who met their untimely demise

From this dark cloud of ill, we found light
That will continue guiding us through life’s flight

The Plight of 4V4V

It caught us off guard
A virus that hit hard
First responders including paramedics
Fight and hope to win this huge pandemic
Depression and confusion set in
People chanted their own philosophies
From panic and growing weary
It could be seen in their actions
It could be heard in their voices
How our lives and economy froze
This period offered an enormous blow
However, during this struggle
We may have to be far away
But together strong we will stay

Your friends feel the effects of what is going on in today's world – look to them and offer each other condolences.

Whatever sadness you feel due to the Contagion, **others feel it too.**

You cannot run to other locations as they have restrictions in place just as there are in your town of residence.

What a Time We Are in

It had been over a century
A plague that could have let us be
Medical experts made it a memory
A different ill brought another treachery
Innocent bystanders unsure of the future
Or if there will ever be one to nurture
'Coz things experts say seem like bloopers
A state of stupor as details look butchered
Wear a mask! No, masks rarely help
Sanitize! No, sanitizers are not good
Some say open so they can make money
Others say opening too soon sounds clumsy
Leadership is needed more than ever
Someone to offer initiatives that are clever
Because social distancing has worn its course
And trying to govern others is no longer in force

Faceless Society

What do you see?
My face or personality
When masks are all
That flow free
Nevertheless, I am still me
Cooperation is key
For this to be temporary
I hope we can let things be
How do I see you?
I hope you are not blue
Knowing masks
Are helping get us through
I do not want you with any flu
We are on the same crew
As we wait for a breakthrough
Let us be each other's guru

A Strange World

A strange world we live in
Things just look so grim
Fans at sports games
Are few and far between
Confused, I am at a dilemma
Dang it! I just wanna go to the cinema
With my friends like before
But we know it's vital staying home
Watching people shopping is a relief
Not seeing many shoppers causes grief
This situation has made life a bore
No one knows what to think or do anymore
Strange world you need to hit the door

Negative News Bureau

This viewer no longer
Supports your narrative
Because it's negative
The deaths are all we hear about
This plague causes daily
Those who left us lived bravely
Guess what I am getting at is
The virus may not be the only cause
Underlying conditions
You want to pause
The epidemic is real
For those affected I kneel
And pray for them to heal
Others are troubled so I feel
Be fair and report everything is my appeal

Balance

Opposites attract
Yes, that is a fact
It is how we find
Common ground
To balance things out

Fearless Society

Being fearless is not scary
Of masks I am an adversary
I know you worry I may catch ills
Thank you for your concern
People think I am being political
But my point is critical
If I feel I am losing my freedom
I fight so I do not become defeated
There are hazards involved
Mental, physical, and beyond
We should let this be a bygone
And wake up to a new dawn
We may be on opposite sides
Think your way I will think mine
But let us unite and take strides

Rona Stress and Protests

First came the pandemic
Unreal like a gimmick
Item rationing and limits
Made people less than cordial
We embraced a new normal
Protective measures were inconsistent
Social distancing no longer exists
As a worldwide public execution
Caused by abuse of power and racism
Set off protests and commotion
Desired is compassion through fairness
A legislation where citizens find success
Because none of us are perfect
Hate is either learned or inbred
But we must display intellect
And keep racism out of the public
Unfortunately, it WILL NEVER go away
Now, it is the hope of many
That both evils will know defeat
For the nation to get back on its feet

What to Do

A boring day to wake up to
Restrictions make for less to do
Feeling like a number in a queue
I get up for some cereal
And gander at the monitor for a view
To see who is going to come through
The same thing! Everyone is feeling blue
What to do? What to do?
Yasss! We're all meeting at the park
Hurry! The nights come sooner than due
Better get ready my mask and hairdo
Share tidbits and see what everyone is up to
Before sleeping ahead of morning's dew

The Weight

Geez! This quarantine
Must have gained at least fifteen
Gyms closed to keep germ free
Salons shut I need hair coloring
The weight I do not need
Some are essentially employed
Others work from home
Instead of being unemployed
The weight no one needs
Little laughing and joking
No bars for beer or chicken wings
No stages for concerts or dancing
With the infection in an upswing
Are disputes with the media
And who leads
Worry for our generation's offspring
The weight our future does not need

The Stars at Night

The stars at night
Are those who glow bright
Standing alone in this fight
Be it family members, friends
Strangers or acquaintances
They serve as an inspiration
Being strong on the outside
Feeling uncertainty on the inside
Yet continue to abide with pride
The stars at night
Give me reason
To wake up and shine bright

The Good Ol' Times of Yesterday

Beer, pretzels, and gathering around
Could always count on 100+ bound
No matter what was on the big screen
Let me tell ya, it was a party scene
Spirits and good times were flowing
Many inebriated did their crowing
Then suddenly, there was a last call
Two party crashers had the gall
One named Covid, the other 'Rona
Both put our society in a coma
Now this is no laughing matter
But these times need lighthearted chatter
Our enemies may have won for the time being
But we have the final say in our well-being
Meanwhile, go get your snacks and drinks
And whatever else to get you through this kink
Get interactive with friends and family
A good ol' shot will soon defeat this catastrophe

Mama, I'm Scared

I don't miss my homework
It's fun sleeping in late
But I don't know what's going on
My teachers and friends are gone
I feel sad and wanna cry sometimes
I have to wear a mask to go outside
Okay. I'm just bored and want to play
I wish this stuff would just go away
Before I lay down at night, I will pray
That we get to go back to school
Seeing my teachers and friends again
Would be so cool
Still, Mama, I'm scared

Passion Thwarts Isolation

I will do what is necessary
Mask, sanitize, and distance
In support of my fellow citizen
But the human comes out in me that desires
To share a knowledge that is carnal
It is my hope to find a partner
One who shares the same understanding
That will get me through the morning
Because nights during this time
Are long, scary, and boring

Satiny Fun Filled Night

The right masks and gloves
Intoxicating as sensual drugs
Two loving humans
Gently stroking each other's ears
Remove the loops that are near
Off come the face covers
Exposing sexiness beyond the eyes
Time to get a bit naughty
And cover each other's bodies
With sanitizer as a shimmery goo
Massaging every inch of skin thru and thru
Both bodies clean and satiny smooth
Laughing and tussling round and round
Appreciating each other's playground
Before caving into their guilty pleasures
Finally! Enjoying heavily sought treasures
Time now to rest alongside the moonlight
And part ways at the alarm of daylight

Death of Friday Nights

Past falls were a ball
Pep rallies to deal with rivalries
Friends talking about parties to attend
Whether a win or taking it on the chin
Friday nights kept the young folk stoked
Without injection there is an infection
One that killed Friday night lights
We would have rather stood in the bleachers
And cheered along with the cheerleaders
Watching our team win was a keeper
Now, we choose different paths to survive
Learning online, we close digital divide
As we protest alongside our teachers
To keep the germs from spreading and staying alive

Treat, Not Trick You

Halloween is fun for everyone
Kids, teens, and grown-ups
Costumes show no age, yup!
It is exciting to see trick-or-treaters
Be happy with snacks and water
But in choosing not to get treated
Your choice does not make you defeated
I would rather you not succumb
To an illness without a vaccination
Until that happens, I support your wishes
If you decide to receive goodies
I will welcome you surely
No matter what your preference is
Keeping each other safe is top priority

'Tis the Season of Confinement

Anticipating a dreary holiday season
Makes for change through new ideas
Family and friends are concerned
Things may have significantly changed
Look on the bright side
Should holiday gatherings be smaller
Maybe the family dysfunction will also
Snowflakes please drop from the sky
Cold enough the germs in the air die
What wishful thinking
Come Thanksgiving and Christmas dinners
May we be guaranteed the tastes and smells of
Apples and cinnamon in the sky through pies
And cloves from turkey and ham in the stove
One thing for sure is
Holiday dinners surrounded by friends and family
Stand the test of time even during a pandemic

Maskerade Not

Mask up, mask down
Up, down, and all around
We're all disgusted with the woes
Brought on by version 2.0
It did produce many heroes
Essential and front-line
They worked hard and shined
Without considering the bottom line
Mental and physical restrictions
Some cannot or will not wear masks
And without those germs can spread fast
So then, why should we follow this half-ass task?
Let us not turn pettiness into worry, fuss, or fight
Masks are trendy – bandanas, neck gaiters, or face protectors
Wear them as part of your attire and unite

Dear High School Seniors

Lost were those last few months
Needed for making many memories
Before heading off in different directions
It is with hope that the underclass students
Heed your guidance and display prudence
As they move forward in the online world

Unfair Departing

A loved one has passed
Social restrictions cause an impasse
Celebrations of life and funeral services
Almost non-existent, this virus is merciless
No funeral is too much for you and me
The pain and grief from not having the peace
Given when witnessing and giving testimony
In honor of loved ones who are deceased
Hopeful we are the spread will slow
That people can have closure

My Damned Experience

Tested positive
Fever 100.3 and 77% oxygen
A loss of taste and smell
Ended up in the hospital
Five days I lie in perspective
Being humble while others were worse
Coming home I take the high road
Honoring those who let me fight
Some awaited their new journey
While others continue being sturdy
Strong at heart, weak in the body
My advocacy
Is just beginning
Zinc, D3, C
And other vitamins
Drinking hot liquids
Eating soups and broths
Nutrition is vital
Just as sunlight and deep breaths
Medicines and remedies keep you going
Quite the caregiver
My husband is

His devotion and allegiance
Give me the lift
To get better so I can fight another day
And inform fellow neighbors and citizens
That we do not have to fear this plague
But meet it head on through knowledge
Go wear your masks just awhile longer
Continue washing your hands and distance
With these practices and a vaccine on the way
We will have a new era of hope and promise YAY!

Top of the New Year

Bottoms up
Tip that cup
We handled a year that was a dud
Lockdowns made many feel
Locked up
Without a heads up
Congrats to all with their heads held high
Including you, this gal, that guy
And all those in between
Remain practicing your hygiene
To a level that this scene is forever unseen

Self-Proclaimed Counselor

A new strain brings a new pain
Whether mental or physical
This virus is like criminal
As many lives were lost
Friends and family
Ask my advice
Worried what
They will have to sacrifice
Please trust a Higher Power I say
One to whom you can pray
The Power wants Its followers
To fear It, yet have faith in It
Question is
How do we balance
Fear and faith?
Fear those
Not heeding safety measures
Plea for hope
We will be clean
Have faith
A Light will shine
On those

Under this destructive spell
This is my best advice
For us to get well
Practicing it, one may become hopeful

Fresh, Open Eyes

Time to shear the old
And anticipate the new
Peel open your eyes
Realize
A vaccine alone
Will not keep us alive
Maybe a five-year window
Might break us from this woe
Scientists and other experts
Need to design and maintain
Protocols
Of the shot
Which are quite a lot
Couldn't come soon enough
As we're all fraught
Crap! What this caused
Until the time we open again comes
We must be cautious
But still have fun

Time to Hangout

Hey buddy
What say
We hangout
Without a doubt
Just because
We are in a drought
We'll go to the hangout
A round of pool and beer
Celebrate our friendship
With some cheer
No bad intentions meant
We need no masks
We may look like fools
People mad, think we're
Breaking rules
While playing pool
Understand
Celebrations are in order
In this time of disorder
Don't worry
Soon we shall scurry
Now satisfied with

This somewhat
Sense of normalcy

Thanks! Markets and Eateries

Owners, Managers, and Staff
Food caterers and deliverers
We should get your autographs
You all continue to save us
Whether we are sick
And under quarantine
Maybe choose not to
Step out on the scene
Or out of the right things
To make a family dish
We will order and meet curbside
But always thanks for coming by
Excited to meet up again
When it comes to food
You all reign

Dark Times

Got a confession
These times
Give me depression
Maybe it's the interaction
We are limited
That makes me feel bad
Maybe it was the hoarding
Of necessities
It sucks to be prohibited
That made me quite mad
Had a friend in the hospital
Not able to see her
My heart bled
It made me extremely sad
Emotions in my mind prickling
Like goosebumps
Running thru my body
Nevertheless
I must keep going
Help has
Got to be out there
To keep me growing

In a post-pandemic era
understand that **you got through** a tough time
standing proud and having more knowledge
than ever to move forward and that **you have**
the strength to be resilient than ever before.

Coloring books, crossword puzzles, magazines, books, household chores.
There is always something to keep you occupied.

Call, text, mail, email, and video chat – **use all communications**
To contact with **friends and family**.

Be hopeful. Think positive. Stay safe.